D0561576

For
Angela, Si—
Christmas love 1993
from
Mary Claire

The
TWELVE DAYS
of
Christmas

By Martin Marix-Evans

PETER PAUPER PRESS, INC.
WHITE PLAINS · NEW YORK

Illustrations copyright ©
Lipton Export Limited 1982

Text copyright © 1993
Peter Pauper Press, Inc.
202 Mamaroneck Avenue
White Plains, NY 10601
All rights reserved
ISBN 0-88088-780-X
Printed in Hong Kong
7 6 5 4 3 2 1

THE TWELVE DAYS OF CHRISTMAS

Mid-winter festivals seem to meet some fundamental human need. Yule, in Northern Europe, was an affirmation of life and the relationship with the environment. Roman Saturnalia was a time of feasting, excess, and the suspension of normal social

restraints. Such indulgence
was not approved by the
fathers of the early Christian
church; Christmas itself was
not recognized before the
4th Century, and in the
twelve days following that
are celebrated in the carol,
medieval society held on to
many earlier traditions.

Christmas has come and
gone and come again as a
festival over the centuries.

The twelve days were the only vacation in medieval England, but by Georgian times even Christmas Day was an ordinary working day. Alabama was—in 1836—the first American state to declare Christmas a holiday. Oklahoma did so in 1890.

The origins of the carol are not known. It appears in many versions throughout

Europe, including a French rendering in which ten of the twelve gifts are food or drink! The traditional tune is repeated with each added gift, until the fifth day, when a variation takes over. The music given here therefore covers gifts one to six, and is consistent thereafter.

The Twelve Days Of Christmas

Four — col-ly birds, three French hens
Two — tur-tle doves, And a part-ridge —
in a pear tree. _____ On the sixth day of
Christ-mas, my true love gave to me.
Six geese a-lay-ing, Five gold — rings---

(Each succeeding verse, or number, has the same
tune as number 6, after which the song proceeds
from 5 down to the end as above.)

7 swans a-swimming . . .   10 drummers drumming
8 maids a-milking   11 Lords a-leaping
9 pipers piping   12 Ladies dancing

*O*n the first day of Christmas
My true love gave to me
A partridge in a pear tree.

December 26

A perfect gift for the first day of the vacation! Not just the main dish, partridge, but the makings of the garnish as well.

Partridge has long been considered a great delicacy. The story is told of the confessor to a King of France who took his sovereign to task on account

of the great number of his
mistresses. Challenged by
the King to declare his
favorite dish, the prelate
nominated partridge. And
the King ordered that he
should be served partridge
every day.

The prelate soon complained:
Perdrix, toujours perdrix
(partridge, always partridge!)
Indeed, remarked the
monarch, *some variety is to be
desired!*

*O*n the second day of Christmas
My true love gave to me
Two turtle doves
And a partridge in a pear tree.

December 27

As a symbol of love and constancy, the turtle dove has a long history. Small and slim, with a beautiful pink breast, it not only looks the part, but also shows a touching affection for its mate.

The pair given in this English song must have

overcomes any slight fault
of translation.

*My beloved spake, and said unto
me, Rise up, my love, my fair
one, and come away.*

*For, lo, the winter is past, the
rain is over and gone;*

*The flowers appear on the earth;
the time of the singing of birds is
come, and the voice of the turtle
is heard in our land;*

The fig tree putteth forth her green figs, and the vines with tender grape give a good smell. . . Arise, my love, my fair one, and come away. (Song of Solomon 2:10-13).

December 28

If these hens are indeed the birds it is natural to assume, the significance of the gift is difficult to understand. Of course they may just be for laying eggs for the beloved's breakfast, or destined for the oven.

What is more likely is that the hens are not birds at all, but stone bottles.

Both Yule and Saturnalia, the ancient mid-winter festivals that contribute so much to the medieval Christmas, were times of great feasting and, to the discomfort of the fathers of the church, drunkenness. St. Gregory Nazianzen, in 389 AD, condemned . . . *feasting to excess, dancing . . .* and such heathen practices as decorating the house with evergreens.

On the fourth day of Christmas
My true love gave to me
Four colly birds
Three French hens
Two turtle doves
And a partridge in a pear tree.

of four and twenty black-birds was no fantasy, and *Old King Cole* also gives an accurate picture of the times. King Cole himself was probably a 3rd Century prince of the former Roman city of Colchester in eastern England, and the song agrees very nicely with the celebration of Christmas. The bowl was for drinking, the pipe for making music (tobacco was unknown until Sir Walter Raleigh acquired the weed from native Americans) and a merry, merry time had he!

December 30

The giving of a ring is an act
of special significance in our
culture today, and so it has
been since earliest times.
Weddings, betrothals and
membership in clubs,
fraternities, and sororities
are sanctified in this way.

The roundness of the ring,
its characteristic of having
no beginning and no end,

symbolizes eternity—the never-changing nature of the commitment it records. The substance of the ring also has meaning. Gold represents supreme value, the gift of wisdom from above.

Our perception of the meaning of the gold ring is much narrower than that of the Middle Ages. Pope Innocent III sent four gold rings as a gift to King John of England. They represented the four virtues of a monarch: justice, fortitude, prudence, and temperance. These were qualities notably lacking in a recipient who was best known for obliging his barons to enforce the signature of Magna Carta to curb his autocratic rule. But the validity of the symbolism remains.

And the fifth ring? What else but love?

*O*n the sixth day of Christmas
My true love gave to me
Six geese a-laying
Five gold rings
Four colly birds
Three French hens
Two turtle doves
And a partridge in a pear tree.

December 31

The goose is a fine gift for anybody. These, of the sixth day, are clearly not intended to be eaten, for they are a-laying, and very fine eggs they give, particularly for making cakes.

The farmyard goose of Old England was not far removed from its ancestor, the greylag goose. This native of the British Isles is still held in respect today because of its characteristics of devotion, intelligence and marital fidelity. It is very probable that they mate for life.

Geese are strongly territorial birds. Alert for any sign of unwelcome guests, they set up a loud cackling should a stranger appear.

Sustenance, security and fidelity—all in one bird: a fine gift, indeed.

On the seventh day of Christmas
My true love gave to me
Seven swans a-swimming
Six geese a-laying
Five gold rings
Four colly birds
Three French hens
Two turtle doves
And a partridge in a pear tree.

January 1

The swan was a bird held in much respect in the Middle Ages. The symbol of Apollo, Greek god of the arts and of prophesy, it was more generally seen as signifying the spirit of poetry. In Celtic lore swans were guardians of departed souls, while Norse belief held that the three fates were symbolized by swans.

A swan received as a gift, however, was much more likely to be perceived (and valued) as a potential meal.

Swan is rarely eaten today, but was quite commonly served to Queen Victoria, with a stuffing of steak and onions and a sauce made of port and red-currant jelly.

The diarist Parson Wood-forde recorded on January

18, 1780, when served swan:

I never eat a bit of swan before, and I think it good eating with a sweet sauce. The swan was killed three weeks before it was eat and yet not the least bad taste of it.

It was also on New Year's Day that gifts were given. A gift from a retainer to his Lord was a form of homage, and from Lord to retainer a symbol of obligation. Many of the poorest people would depend on gifts of food for survival at this hard time of year. Gifts at Christmas did not become usual until the 19th Century, and in the Netherlands, for example, it is still the custom to give presents on St. Nicholas's Day, well before Christmas.

On the eighth day of Christmas
My true love gave to me
Eight maids a-milking
Seven swans a-swimming
Six geese a-laying
Five gold rings
Four colly birds
Three French hens
Two turtle doves
And a partridge in a pear tree.

January 2

The great Christmas holiday released laborers from the heavy work in the fields, but the everyday tasks of caring for the farm animals still had to be done. And besides, a medieval lord would show vast hospitality to mark his wealth and position, and all that cooking demanded a supply of milk, cream and butter.

The Duke of Buckingham entertained 182 people for Christmas dinner in 1507 and a further 319 on the last day of the holiday!

Apart from butter and cheese, milk provided the chief ingredients of White Pots, a dish akin to both a soufflé and a baked custard. The milk was slowly added to beaten eggs, and the beating-in continued with flavorings such as rose or orange water, nutmeg, and sugar. Then came the cream. The mixture was poured into a dish lined with thin slices of bread, topped with butter, and baked.

The meal might also be brought to a close with a syllabub—cream whipped into a mixture of lemon juice, sugar and liquor.

With custards and other dishes depending on the dairy, even eight maids to do the milking might not have been enough!

On the ninth day of Christmas
My true love gave to me
Nine pipers piping
Eight maids a-milking
Seven swans a-swimming
Six geese a-laying
Five gold rings
Four colly birds
Three French hens
Two turtle doves
And a partridge in a pear tree.

January 3

When we speak of pipers today, a vision of the swirl of kilted Highlanders is summoned up, and the plaintive theme and drone of the pipes is set against the purple heather of the wild Scottish hills. The association of the bagpipes with the New Year is reinforced by the precedence given by the Scots to

Hogmanay over Christmas itself.

It is unlikely that the Twelve Days of Christmas conjured up any such images for medieval listeners. Pipe, to them, would mean a flute.

The origin of the pipe is lost in pre-history. It is one of the simplest musical instruments known, easily fashioned by the poorest people, but also capable of great sophistication. As an instrument to make music for dancing it suited all levels of society. The holidays were celebrated with games and dancing, so having a gift of flautists would be a fine present, and rather more congenial to have in the house of a cold winter's night than a bevy of bagpipes.

And, of course, the gift of pipers also placed the recipient in command of the revels—for he who pays the piper calls the tune!

On the tenth day of Christmas
My true love gave to me
Ten drummers drumming
Nine pipers piping
Eight maids a-milking
Seven swans a-swimming
Six geese a-laying
Five gold rings
Four colly birds
Three French hens
Two turtle doves
And a partridge in a pear tree.

January 4

The noise of ten drummers would not be welcome in the house! But it was not for indoor use that they were given, for this is the season of Wassail.

Evil spirits, as everybody knows, cannot abide loud and sudden noises. To shout, clap your hands, fire your guns in the air, all are

instinctive ways of cele-
brating and making all
secure. The mid-winter
festival is also a time to
affirm the certainty of a
subsequent spring and the
healthy growth of new
crops.

Wassail is derived from the
Anglo-Saxon meaning
"good health." The cere-
mony it is chiefly associated
with—still performed in

parts of England—is the safeguarding of the cider apple trees.

All sorts of variants of wassail are recorded, but the basics are consistent. A young person, boy or girl depending on locality, is carried in ceremony round the apple orchards to put a cider-soaked fragment of bread in the crook of the branches while cider is poured at the base of the tree. Loud noises are part of the ceremony—these days the sound of shotguns being discharged. Before the days of firearms, drums would meet the need.

On the eleventh day of
Christmas
My true love gave to me
Eleven Lords a-leaping
Ten drummers drumming
Nine pipers piping
Eight maids a-milking
Seven swans a-swimming
Six geese a-laying
Five gold rings
Four colly birds
Three French hens
Two turtle doves
And a partridge in a pear tree.

January 5

During the Twelve Days, a
holiday from the cold, wet,
and heavy work of the
winter countryside, there
was a relaxation of the
ordinary rules of behavior
that regulated the highly
structured society of medieval
England. This tradition
owes much to the ancient
Roman festival of Saturnalia,
when a Lord of Misrule was

appointed. Other customs from the same source were cross-dressing, which led to the convention of the Christmas pantomime where the hero is played by an actress and the Dame by an actor, and dressing in the skins of animals.

These leaping Lords could be members of the aristocracy taking full part in the festivities, but they are just as likely to be servants spared their regular duties to strut as rulers for a short time.

The inversion of social roles survives to this day in the British Army, where it is customary at Christmastime for the officers to serve a meal to the "men."

The most extreme example of the temporary promotion

of the humble to high rank
was in the appointment of
boy bishops. They held
office from St. Nicholas's
Day, December 6, until the
end of Christmas, and were
dressed in full regalia,
performing public duties
(with the exception of
saying Mass) just like real
bishops. If a boy died in
office, he was buried with
all the honors that would be
accorded a full bishop.

On the twelfth day of
     Christmas
My true love gave to me
Twelve Ladies dancing
Eleven Lords a-leaping
Ten drummers drumming
Nine pipers piping
Eight maids a-milking
Seven swans a-swimming
Six geese a-laying
Five gold rings
Four colly birds
Three French hens
Two turtle doves
And a partridge in a pear tree.

January 6

This is the last day of the
medieval Christmas vacation,
Twelfth Night. The Christian
church adopted the day as
Epiphany, the day on which
the Holy Child was first
presented to people who
were not Jews. The story of
the Three Kings or Magi
was associated with this day
to bring the holiday to a
religious close. By tradition

this is also the day when the decorations of evergreen branches and fir trees are removed from the house to avert bad luck.

The final opportunity for making merry was not to be missed. As late as 1668 the great diarist, Samuel Pepys, records Twelfth Night in London as follows:

... a very good supper and mighty merry and good music playing; and after supper to dancing and singing ... till about 2 in the morning; and then broke up ... and so away to bed, weary and mightily pleased ...

The Twelve Days of Christmas embodies beliefs fundamental to humankind: acceptance of the essential rhythms of nature, joy in the gift of life, and, greatest of all, the act of giving as an expression of love.

And so the holiday comes
to an end!

Peace and love be with you.

The illustrations are reproduced by courtesy of the Lipton Tea Company. They were commissioned for a limited edition of special tea caddies to celebrate the Christmas season, and each contained one of Lipton's superb blends of fine tea. The pictures are the work of English artist Carol Lawson.